Butterfly or Moth?

How Do You Know?

Melissa Stewart

Enslow Elementary
an imprint of
Enslow Publishers, Inc.
40 Industrial Road
Box 398
Berkeley Heights, NJ 07922
USA
http://www.enslow.com

Contents

Words to Know

antennae (an **TEN** ee)—Two structures on the head of insects and some other animals. They help animals sense the world around them.

chrysalis (**KRIS** uh liss)—The hard outer skin on a butterfly pupa.

cocoon (kuh **KOON**)—The silky case spun by a moth caterpillar. The moth pupa lives in it while it changes into an adult insect.

insect (**IN** sekt)—An animal with three body parts and six legs. Most insects have two pairs of wings.

predator (**PREH** duh tur)—An animal that hunts and kills other animals for food.

pupa (**PYOO** puh)—The third part in the life cycle of some insects. A pupa changes into an adult.

scale (skayl)—One of the thin, flat, skinlike plates that cover the wings of butterflies and moths.

Do You Know?

Which of
these insects
is a butterfly?
Which one is
a moth?
Do you know?

Knobs or No Knobs?

Eastern tiger swallowtail butterfly

A butterfly has two antennae for smelling. They are long and thin. Each one has a round knob on the end.

A moth's antennae are short and feathery. They help a moth smell and fly.

Eggar moth

Day or Night?

Most butterflies fly during the day. They rest at night.

Ulysses butterfly

Spurge hawk moth

Most moths fly at night. They rest during the day.

Smooth or Fuzzy?

A butterfly has a thin, smooth coat of scales on its wings.

High brown fritillary butterfly scales

A moth
has a thick,
fuzzy coat of scales.
The thick coat helps
the moth stay
warm at night.

Luna moth wing

Closed or Open?

A butterfly rests with its wings closed. On cool mornings, a butterfly spreads its wings to soak up sunlight.

Birdwing butterfly

Melanic peppered moth

A moth rests with its wings open.

13

Bright or Dull?

Common bluebottle
butterfly

Most butterflies
have bright wings.
The colors can attract
mates. They can help
the butterfly blend in
with flowers. They can
even warn predators
to stay away.

Tau emperor moth

Most moths
are brown or gray.
Their dull colors help
them hide while they
rest during the day.

Chrysalis or Cocoon?

A butterfly has four parts to its life cycle. They are egg, caterpillar, pupa, and adult. A pupa hangs from a branch or a stem. A hard skin called a chrysalis protects it.

Monarch butterfly chrysalis

Polyphemus moth cocoon

A moth has four life stages, too. A moth pupa usually lies on or under the ground. A cocoon of silk surrounds it.

Now Do You Know?

This insect flies during the day.

It has bright, colorful wings.

It has long, thin antennae with knobs on the ends.

Its pupa changes inside a chrysalis.

Monarch butterfly

It rests with its wings closed.

It has thin, smooth scales.

It's a butterfly!

This insect flies at night.

It rests with its wings open.

It has dull, gray wings.

Polyphemus moth

It has short, feathery antennae.

It has a thick, fuzzy coat of scales.

Its pupa changes inside a cocoon.

It's a moth!

What a Surprise!

Most butterflies drink plant juices with long strawlike mouthparts. But they taste with their feet.

Brown skipper butterfly

Elephant hawk moth caterpillar

Some moths do all their eating while they are caterpillars. The adults do not have any mouthparts.

Learn More

Books

Bishop, Nic. *Butterflies and Moths*. New York: Scholastic, 2009.

Mound, Laurence. *Insect*. New York: DK Children, 2007.

Murawski, Darlyne. *Face to Face with Butterflies*. Washington, D.C.: National Geographic, 2010.

Stewart, Melissa. *A Place for Butterflies*. Atlanta, Ga.: Peachtree Publishers, 2006.

Walters, Martin. *The Illustrated World Encyclopedia of Insects*. London: Lorenz Books, 2010.

Web Sites

The Butterfly Website
  http://butterflywebsite.com/

The Children's Butterfly Site
  http://kidsbutterfly.org/

North American Moths
  http://moths.wordpress.com/

Index

Enslow Elementary, an imprint of Enslow Publishers, Inc.

Enslow Elementary® is a registered trademark of Enslow Publishers, Inc.

Library of Congress Cataloging-in-Publication Data

Stewart, Melissa
   Butterfly or moth? : how do you know? / Melissa Stewart.
      p. cm. — (Which animal is which?)
   Includes bibliographical references and index.
   Summary: "Explains to young readers how to tell the difference between butterflies and
      moths"—Provided by publisher.
   Libary Ed. ISBN 978-0-7660-3678-9
   Paperback ISBN 978-1-59845-235-8
   1. Butterflies—Juvenile literature. 2. Moths—Juvenile literature. I. Title.
   QL544.2.S7454 2011
   595.78'9—dc22   2010003276

Printed in the United States of America

102010 Lake Book Manufacturing, Inc., Melrose Park, IL

10 9 8 7 6 5 4 3 2 1

To Our Readers: We have done our best to make sure all Internet Addresses in this book were active and appropriate when we went to press. However, the author and the publisher have no control over and assume no liability for the material available on those Internet sites or on other Web sites they may link to. Any comments or suggestions can be sent by e-mail to comments@enslow.com or to the address on the back cover.

♻ Enslow Publishers, Inc., is committed to printing our books on recycled paper. The paper in every book contains 10% to 30% post-consumer waste (PCW). The cover board on the outside of each book contains 100% PCW. Our goal is to do our part to help young people and the environment too!

Note to Parents and Teachers: The *Which Animal Is Which?* series supports the National Science Education Standards for K–4 science. The Words to Know section introduces subject-specific vocabulary words, including pronunciation and definitions. Early readers may need help with these new words.

Photo Credits: iStockphoto.com: © Greg Gardner, pp. 8, 23, © Henrick Larson, p. 7; Photo Researchers, Inc.: Millard H. Sharp, p. 17, Stephen Dalton, p. 9, Ted Kinsman, p. 11; Shutterstock.com, pp. 1, 2, 3, 4, 5, 6, 10, 12, 13, 14, 15, 16, 18, 19, 20, 21.

Cover Photos: Shutterstock.com